I am Baptized

A Cosmic Event In Your History

I am
Baptized

A Cosmic Event In Your History

RICHARD A. JESPERSEN

Illustrated By:
Brenda Hermundstad Yirsa

ARPress
ILLUMINATING IDEAS,
EMPOWERING VOICES

ARPress
45 Dan Road Suite 36
Canton MA 02021

Hotline: 1(888) 821-0229
Fax: 1(508) 545-7580

Ordering Information:
Quantity Sales. Special discounts are available on quantity purchases by corporations, associations, and others. For details, contact the publisher at the address above.

Printed in the United States of America.

ISBN-13   Paperback   979-8-89330-113-7
             eBook   979-8-89330-115-1
             Hardback   979-8-89330-114-4

Library of Congress Control Number: 2024900574

To my father and mother,
Robert and Laura Jespersen,
who brought me to the water
and put me in the way of the Word.
I am eternally (literally so) grateful.
- Rich Jespersen

To my husband, Ken,
who has stood by me
and encouraged me through
these many years of marriage,
and to my three gifts from God,
Justin, Chris, and Sarah.
More importantly,
I give God the glory
For giving me this gift of creativity.
- Brenda Hermundstad Yirsa

The words are spoken to you;
the water is poured over you;
the promise is given for you:
"You, yes, you,
by name,
are baptized
in the name
of the Father,
and of the Son,
and of the Holy Spirit.
Amen."
It is so!

_____

(name of the baptized)

_____

(date of baptism)

Photo of the baptized

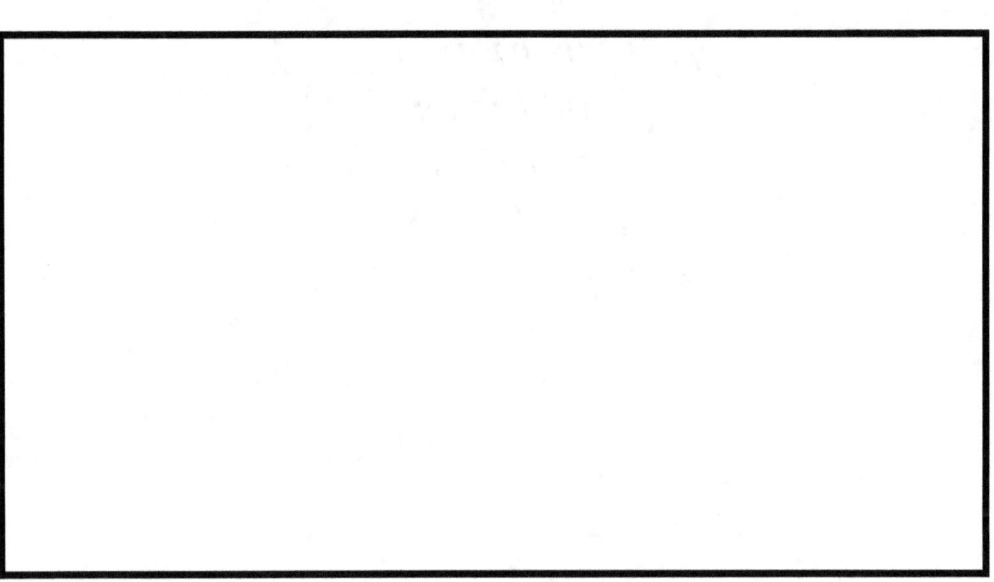

Baptism
is what
God does!

The Church
is
the servant,
the instrument
of this
baptizing God.

The Church is commanded to baptize: "All authority in heaven and earth has been given to me,"
Jesus said. "Go, therefore, and make disciples of all nations, baptizing them in the name of the
Father, and of the Son, and of the Holy Spirit, and teaching them to obey everything that I have
commanded you. And remember, I am with you always to the end of the age." (Matthew 28:18-
20) When something is done under the authority of, at the command of, and with the promise of
someone else, then that someone else, in this case God, Father, Son, and Holy Spirit, is the One doing
the action. God commands the Church to baptize and promises to act where the Church so baptizes.
Who does what in baptism? The parents or sponsors put the person to be baptized in the way of
the water and the words. The congregation, including the parents and sponsors, witness the event
and commit themselves to support the baptized in the life of a Christian disciple. The person to
be baptized, at whatever age, does nothing except stand still long enough to get wet and hear the
promise. The pastor or priest is the messenger, pouring the water and saying the words. God, Father,
Son, and Holy Spirit, baptizes!

1

What does God do in baptism?
In baptism,
God does
what
the water does
and
the Word declares!
With the water,
God
paints a picture,
water
being
the artistic medium.
With the words,
God
gives a promise,
and explains what
this baptism means.
If you want to know
what your baptism means,
follow the water and listen to the Word.

As water is
for washing,
so, God,
in baptism,
washes,
cleanses,
bathes,
forgives.

In Titus 3:5, St. Paul writes that God "saved us, not because of any works of righteousness that we have done, but according to his mercy, through the washing of rebirth and renewal by the Holy Spirit."

Your sins
are forgiven!
You
are forgiven!
Washed
squeaky clean,
inside out clean,
a rainbow
marks your way
from the past into God's
future for you.

As water
quenches thirst,
so, God,
in baptism
quenches
your God-shaped thirst
by the Spirit
within,
a drink of life
from a spring of living water
bubbling upward,
Godward,
and flowing outward,
an en-Spirited life.

Jesus promises: "Those who drink of the water that I will give them will never be thirsty. The water that I will give will become in them a spring of water gushing up to eternal life." (John 4:14) "Let anyone who is thirsty come to me and let the one who believes in me drink. As the scripture has said, 'Out of his heart shall flow rivers of living water.' Now he said this about the Spirit, which believers were to receive...." (John 7:37b-39a)

As water
is great fun
to play in,
so, God,
in baptism,
initiates us
into the most
fun-filled adventure in life,
following Jesus.

As Jesus promises, "I came that they may have life and have it abundantly" (John 10:10) And "I have said these things to you so that my joy may be in you, and that your joy may be complete." (John 15:11)

The baptized
live as children
splashing
in grace,
playing
in the earth-as-garden,
knowing
the great fun
of losing one's life
for Jesus.

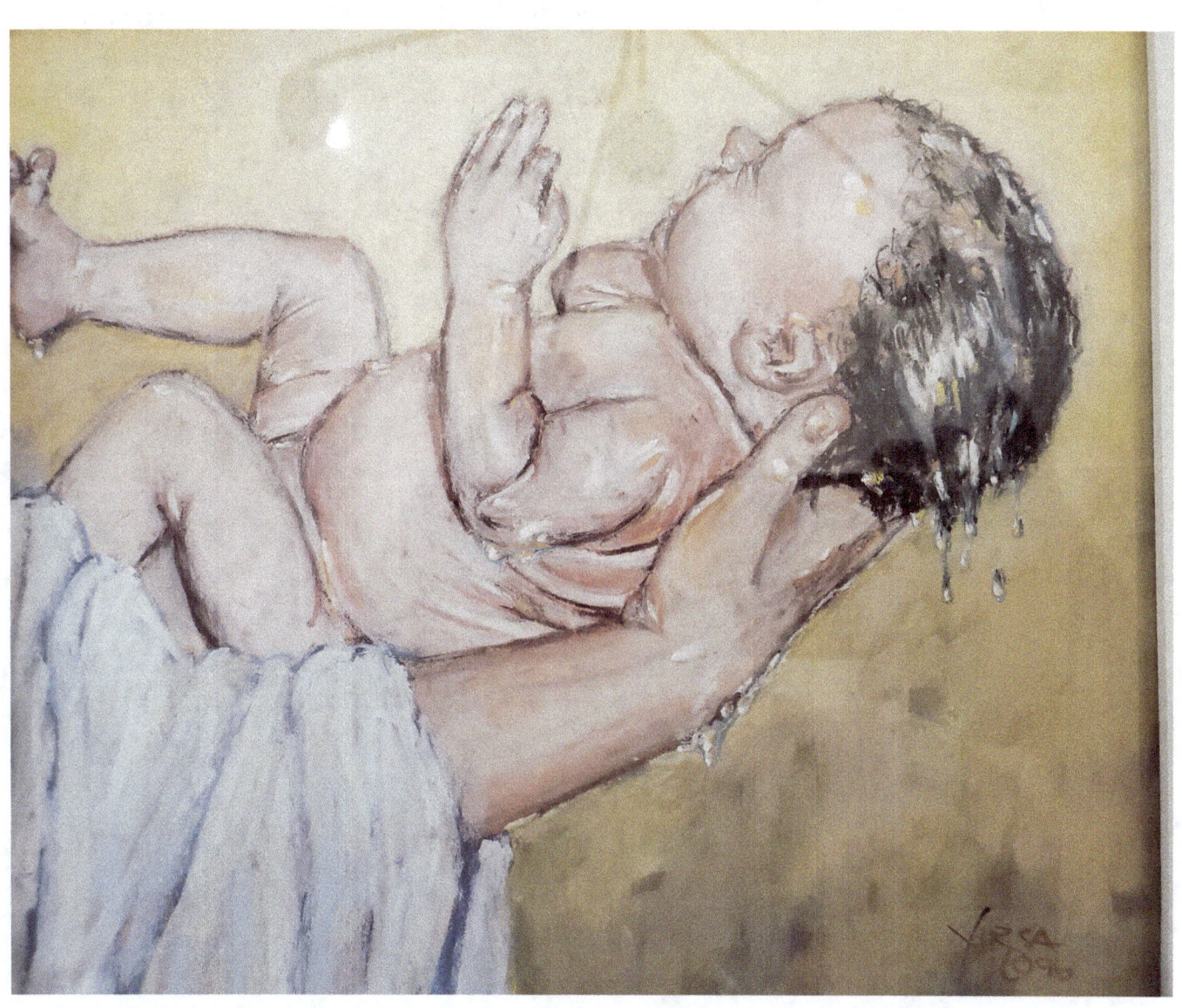

As babies
are born
wet,
so, follow
the water
of baptism
to new birth.

Jesus invites, "Very truly, I tell you, no one can enter the kingdom of God without being born of water and the Spirit.". (John 3:5)

Jesus
did not come
to make good or bad people better,
but to make dead people alive.
Baptism is
a watery new birth
into a life with God,
an act of new creation,
God's kind of play.

Danger!
Baptismal water ahead!
A relentless undertow
of grace,
crosscurrents
pulling us
in over our heads
and out of our depth,
into Christ,
Baptism is
the drowning of the
self-as-God
and the raising of the
self-in-Christ.
God buries
in a watery grace
everything not of God
and raises to new life
everything of God.
Baptism is
our watery
Good Friday
and Easter.

St. Paul writes: "Do you not know that all of us who have been baptized into Christ Jesus were baptized into his death? Therefore, we have been buried with him by baptism into death, so that, just as Christ was raised from the dead by the glory of the Father, so we too might walk in newness of life. For if we have been united with him in a death like his, we will certainly be united with him in a resurrection like his." (Romans 6:3-5)

In water
of all shapes and sizes,
in oceans, lakes, rivers, and streams,
in ponds, pools, and puddles,
we go fishing
for catch of all kinds, shapes, and sizes.
So also
in the waters of baptism,
we go fishing
for people of all kinds, shapes, and sizes,
for God's catch-o'-the-day.

"As (Jesus) walked by the Sea of Galilee, he saw two brothers, Simon, who is called Peter, and Andrew, his brother, casting a net into the sea — for they were fishermen. And he said, 'Follow me, and I will make you fish for people.' Immediately, they left their nets and followed him." (Matthew 4:18-20)
"And Jesus came and said to (the disciples), '…Go therefore and make disciples of all nations, baptizing them….'" (Matthew 28:18a, 19a)

17

To be baptized
is not
a solitary experience,
but a family free-for-all.
We are tossed into the water
with Jesus
and all who are called to be his disciples,
the whole Christian Church on earth,
the whole people of God
of all times and places.
To be baptized
is to belong!

St. Paul writes, "You were baptized into union with Christ, and how you are clothed, so to speak, with the life of Christ himself. So, there is no difference between Jews and Gentiles, between slaves and free people, between men and women; you are all one in union with Christ Jesus." (Galatians 3:27-28)

In water,
we see reflections
of the world as it is.
In baptismal water,
we see reflections
of the world as it will be,
and the changes that are afoot
by God's grace.

"For now, we see in a mirror dimly, but then we will see face to face. Now I know only in part; but then I will know fully, even as I have been fully known." (I Corinthians 13:12)

"Beloved, we are God's children now, what we will be has not yet been revealed. What we do know is this: when (Christ) is revealed, we will be like him, for we will see him as he is. And all who have this hope in him purifies themselves, just as he is pure." (1 John 3:2-3)

"And I am confident of this, that the one who began a good work among us will bring it to completion by the day of Jesus Christ." (Philippians 1:6)

"Not that I have already obtained this or have already reached the goal; but I press on to make it my own, because Christ Jesus has made me his own. Beloved, I do not consider that I have made it my own; but this one thing I do: forgetting what lies behind and straining forward to what lies ahead, I press on toward the goal for the prize of the heavenly call of God in Christ Jesus." (Philippians 3:12-14)

To live the baptized life
is to follow
the way of the water and the Word.
To live baptized
is to walk wet.

If God in baptism washes me clean, forgiving my sins, then to walk wet means to forgive as I have been forgiven. (Ephesians 4;30-32)

If God in baptism quenches my God-shaped thirst with the presence of the Holy Spirit within, then to walk wet means to live in the power of that Spirit and resist the temptations of the world. (Galatians 5:16-26; Philippians 4:4-13)

If God in baptism initiates me into a life of joy, then to walk wet means to discover the joy of losing my life for Jesus. (Luke 9:23-25; Philippians 4:4-9)

If God in baptism births me a new child of the kingdom of God, then to walk wet means to trust with the faith of a child in this God who loves me. (John 3:16; Matthew 18:3)

If God in baptism puts me to death and raises me to newness of life, then to walk wet means to live daily turning from sin to live for God. (Romans 6:6-11)

If in baptism I am caught and made God's own, then I am called to fish for others also, that they too might be likewise caught by such grace. (Matthew 4:19)

If God in baptism joins me to the forever family of God, then to walk wet means to learn to love others as I have been loved and declare the good news of God's love to the whole world. (John 15:12; 1 Peter 2:9-10)

If God in baptism has begun something, I am called to reject despair and live in confidence that God will complete what has been begun. (Philippians 1:6; 3:12-13)

If God, through the Church, baptizes me in the name of the Father, and of the Son, and of the Holy Spirit, then I am among God's own elect people and live in obedience to all that Christ has commanded the Church, trusting in Christ's promised presence for the power of Christian discipleship. (Matthew 28:18-20)

"Thus, a Christian life is nothing else than a daily Baptism, once begun and ever continued."

(Martin Luther, Large Catechism, The Book of Concord, Fortress Press, Tappert Edition, 1959, p.445)

To live baptized
is to live out
the baptismal renunciation:
"Do you renounce
all the forces of evil, the devil, and all his empty promises?"
I do.
and the baptismal affirmation:
"Do you believe in God the Father?"
I believe in God the Father almighty, creator of heaven and earth.
Do you believe in Jesus Christ, the Son of God?
I believe in Jesus Christ, his only Son, our Lord.
He was conceived by the power of the virgin Mary.
He suffered under Pontius Pilate, was crucified, died, and was buried.
He descended into hell.
On the third day, he rose again.
He ascended into heaven and is seated at the right hand of the Father.
He will come again to judge the living and the dead.
Do you believe in God the Holy Spirit?
I believe in the Holy Spirit,
the holy catholic church, the communion of saints, the forgiveness of sins,
the resurrection of the body, and the life everlasting.
Amen.

You are baptized
into this living faith,
the faith of the church,
passed by the apostles themselves
through the generations of baptized to us,
a great continuum
of baptismal command and promise.

You are baptized
set afloat
on the great river
of God's grace
toward the world,
equipped with
what has been believed in the church
everywhere,
and always,
and by everyone.

I,
therefore,
in faith,
simply receive
what God does in baptism!
I do not
and cannot
add to,
only live in and live out
what God does.
I live
by faith
in this God
who has baptized me!
Affirming my baptism,
I do nothing,
but simply
let be done
what has been done.
I go with the flow
of God's baptismal doing.
I am baptized!
Amen!
So be it!
Thanks be to God!

(From Martin Luther's Small Catechism)

The Sacrament of Holy Baptism
in the plain form in which the head of the family shall teach it to his household.

First

What is baptism? Answer: Baptism is not merely water, but it is water used according to God's command and connected with God's Word.

What is this Word of God? Answer: As recorded in Matthew 28:19, our Lord Christ said, "Go therefore and make disciples of all nations, baptizing them in the name of the Father and of the Son and of the Holy Spirit."

Second

What gifts or benefits does Baptism bestow? Answer: It effects forgiveness of sins, delivers from death and the devil, and grants eternal salvation to all who believe, as the Word and promise of God declare.

What is this Word and promise of God? Answer: As recorded in Mark 16:16, our Lord Christ said, "He who believes and is baptized will be saved; but he who does not believe will be condemned."

Third

How can water produce such great effects? Answer: It is not the water that produces these effects, but the Word of God connected with the water, and our faith which relies on the Word of God connected with the water. For without the Word of God, the water is merely water and no Baptism. But when connected with the Word of God it is a Baptism, that is, a gracious water of life and a washing of regeneration and renewal in the Holy Spirit, as St. Paul wrote to Titus (Titus 3:5-8): "He saved us by the washing of regeneration and renewal in the Holy Spirit, which he poured out upon us richly through Jesus Christ our Savior, so that we might be justified by his grace and become heirs in hope of eternal life. The saying is sure."

Fourth

What does such baptizing with water signify? Answer: It signifies that the old Adam in us, together with all sins and evil lusts, should be drowned by daily sorrow and repentance and be put to death, and that the new man should come forth daily and rise up, cleansed and righteous, to live forever in God's presence.

Where is this written? Answer: In Romans 6:4, St. Paul wrote, "We were buried therefore with him by baptism into death, so that as Christ was raised from the dead by the glory of the Father, we too might walk in newness of life."